Paddle Your Kayak

Paddle Your Kayak

The thoughts and Poems of an Old Fogey

By O.L.D.Fogey

iUniverse, Inc.
New York   Bloomington

iUniverse books may be ordered through booksellers or by contacting:

iUniverse
1663 Liberty Drive
Bloomington, IN 47403
www.iuniverse.com
1-800-Authors (1-800-288-4677)

ISBN: 978-1-4401-3606-1 (sc)
ISBN: 978-1-4401-3815-7 (ebook)

Printed in the United States of America

iUniverse rev. date: 06/10/2009

For my Family

Past, Present and Future

But uglier yet is the hump we get from having too little to do.

Rudyard Kipling 1865-1935

Preface

It is said that writing poetry is good for your health and being a retired teacher of English literature who wished to look after his well being I decided to see if my style of verse would keep me away from the doctors. Ten years along this particular road and I'm still thinking as I did while writing my first poem. What right have I, an ordinary bloke, to act like a competent Wordsmith? It took me three attempts to pass G.C.E English Literature back in '64, although I must admit in my early teens I loved to read. I wasn't overly keen on Betjeman whom I found as attractive as bitumen and Frost left me cold. I preferred Biggles to Bill Shakespeare. Fortunately academics in my later school years managed to instill an appreciation of English literature in me. Though I am sure even they would have raised an eyebrow at this pupil finishing his working life as Head of Education at a school for children with emotional and behavioural problems. My father gave me my first poem to learn. It was Kipling's The Camels Hump and I would like to think I might follow the poet's style if I cannot match his quality. As with most poets the subject matter for my poetry comes from experiences I have encountered. So what follows are reminiscences in rhyme of events in an ordinary life. A life in which the poetry suggests I paddled my kayak, did not drift with the tide and yes it has helped me stay away from the doctors.

O.L.D. Fogey

Contents

Introduction

Paddle Your Kayak is the author's euphemism for 'get up off your backside and make things happen.' Seven chapters span 50 years in what Fogey considers to be an ordinary life. A fogey, by the way, being a dull, old fellow with antiquated views. Yet as you read your way through the verse, was it such an unassuming life? Poems such as That's life, Sad Waters, First Contact, My fallen Friend, suggest this person paddled their kayak rather than drifted with the tide. From the experiences he encountered came what he calls his Thoughts (at the beginning of each chapter), which he also voices in To Die or Not to Die, Ode to the would be Hack and The Man from Texas. The topics Old Fogey has chosen to write on are ones that have created an impact on his life. Family, countryside, children, growing old, memories and his dislikes. Hopefully this book will allow the reader to relax and reflect and find the poetry often amusing, sometimes sad, maybe annoying and always moreish.

First Thought.

From me to you.

Any moment in life can be a point of reference

But on your demise will you leave thinking; "did I make a difference."

Was there some time in your life on this Earth

That you made people think or even cry out with mirth.

Did anyone learn from what you had to offer?

Or did it always go in one ear and out of the other.

So when the time comes, just before you truly depart

Don't let your only legacy be the last sigh from your heart.

Chapter One

Poems aboutFamily Life.

A Second Thought.

With children and a loving wife

One or all can give you strife

But no matter what they do

Support them, love them, they are yours for life

The School Run

It takes fifty minutes to do the school run

Every day a commitment to deliver my son

Then on to drop off my wife at the station

And drive my youngest to play group, the final destination.

But if I've learnt another fact of life this year

It's driving in the rush hour traffic, certainly is no cheer,

For getting there as fast as you can

Never works and you just get annoyed at that man

Or woman you have tried to overtake.

Now you can't get back to your lane

So you compound your error with another mistake

And speed up the outside lane to force your way back

Slamming the anchors on when you spot the gap

And veering sharply to get back on the right track.

All you've achieved is to annoy the people around you

Get yourself tensed up

Nearly send your family to a church pew.

So learn the lesson of life don't rush, take your time

Stay at the back, relax, you'll still get there by nine.

Little Treasures

When your child does the unexpected,

And creeps into bed, quite undetected

Nothing can surpass

That sense of deep happiness.

So when you drift out of sleep

And take a little peep

You know the memory will linger

At the bunch of curled fingers

Lying in your palm.

All relaxed and calm,

You can drift back to sleep,

Again.

That's Life

As a young married man I was too busy by far

To think of having children, I'd rather have a car.

At twenty four it was work, all rugby and booze

So no offspring came along to step into my shoes

A couple is two, a family is three

So I got a Siamese cat called Cymbal you see.

But things weren't going well I didn't have the nous

So I left the cat when I left the house.

Having children was something I left till quite late

When Henryk was one month I was thirty eight.

So why at thirty nine did I sire another

Bruno the babe was a laidback little brother

But he'd argue with Henryk,

To each the other was a chore,

Then three year later came Krysztof, one more

And low and behold I was now, forty four.

Jacek the fourth was a blessing from heaven

Even though by now I was forty seven

Bringing up four meant I knew what to expect

But the fifth was Patryk, a challenge, not to reject.

By then I was fifty so I decided to stick

Oh no here comes Maksym and he's number six.

Enough is enough, I went for the chop

At fifty two I decided, don't get caught on the hop.

Noah's Flood 2109

Our home stands in the lee of a hill

Great granddad left it to us in his will.

It looks west across the lowlands of south Devon

Now it's an island, one of seven.

Once it looked over fields and trees

Now water before us is all one sees.

The ice caps melted, the Gulf Stream ceased to flow,

Sea levels rose and I inherited a waterside bungalow.

Homes down the slope did not fare so well

A saltwater immersion became their death knell.

Still they play their part as a tourist attraction

Only it's with scuba divers they now have their interaction

In Granddads day people warned, said what they could

That ice caps would melt, there would be a Noah Flood.

But Nations polluted the atmosphere, ignored what was said

And people of the lowlands before the creeping tide fled.

The T.V. Chef.

Mum cooks, dad washes up

Rest of them just eat and sup.

Then they depart clearing the table

As least they do as best they 're able.

Dad into the kitchen

Finds devastation,

Pans piled high

No consideration.

Open packets, flour spilt

No remorse and no guilt.

Ask in our kitchen, it 's a fact of life

A mess while cooking is no fault of my wife.

Not that she 's the least bit deaf

My spouse just acts like she 's a TV chef.

Sleep Time

Two in the morning

Here the wife snoring

Hear the cat meowing

Yes the kids are howling

Give a nudge to my wife

Calm the children, end the strife.

Let cat in with eyes that glint,

Mouse in mouth, at the sprint

Drops the mouse, very curious

No! says I, very furious

Creature runs behind the drawers

Cat can't reach it with her paws.

Four in the morning

Again the wife is snoring

And the cats meowing

Yes the kids are howling

Now the mouse is calling;

Life is never boring.

continued

Sleep Time (continued)

Scared the mouse from behind the radiator

Cat loved it, became the terminator

Shooed feline with mouse out two minutes later

Shuffled off to the loo for a call of nature

Back to bed after my wee

But where there was one human

There are now three.

Six in the morning

Yes my wife has stopped her snoring

But my child who sleeps perpendicular

Has just kicked me in the testicular

And all wake up from their doze

To find dad stricken in the fetal pose.

The Cartoon Viewer.

I can't hear my cartoon says our youngest

To the builders knocking out beams

Encrusted with fungus.

Six weeks upstairs to build bedrooms anew

Means five boys in one bedroom which leads onto -phew,

Baths every night, clean clothes every morning,

and no apples for Krys

Decreases the farting if not the yawning.

There's a plea before nine and then after four

For the urchins to see bedrooms

Grow out of the floor.

No you can't go up there, don't play on the stairs,

Stay clear of the scaffolding- what a nightmare.

Builders have tea at ten, one and four,

They must get their dosage, we don't want them sore.

Sound navvies they are and earning their bob

Working quite hard and doing a good job.

But some day there's more builders, and others there's fewer

To listen to the moans of a young cartoon viewer.

Chapter Two

Poems about Our Countryside

A third thought.

This island is but a vessel

Holding jewels very special

Our countryside reflects our essence

For this we should be prepared to wrestle.

The Exhausted Fox

On the high banks of the lane spread a carpet of purple,

The entrance to the den concealed under the roots of a tree.

I saw the red coats on the hill, expectant, keen to be hurtful,

Where was the fox, terrified, trembling, struggling to go free.

My car moving slowly passed from light into shade

When out jumped the fox almost under my wheel.

Pure fear in its flight, no pause had it made

It vanished so fast, I wondered, was it quite real.

Looking back from the crest, had the pack got it scented,

The fox may escape, the hounds may yet fail.

It looked so one sided could the kill be prevented

Backing down to the den I let my exhaust mask the trail.

The View From my Window

I could be in China or even Kabul

Where peaks and hilltops float on a sea of cotton wool.

Where islands with isolated trees limp and still

In early morning mist hover and appear so tranquil.

It's the view from my window

Where I could be looking out over heaven

But then rain smudges the pane

To remind me I'm actually in Devon.

The Cherry Tree

Autumn winds have blown away your leaves

Fruit decimated, most by winged thieves

Looking forlorn with rings of peeling bark

With tentacle like branches inviting sparrow or lark.

Your fan shaped silhouette backed by a silver grey cloud

Growing so fast, reaches upwards, pleading yet proud.

Visited by magpies, squirrels and jays

Who won't be hidden by leaves until at least come next May.

All lazily watched by the cat on the arbor

Not cherry pie is she thinking will be the fruits of her labour.

Fallapit House.

(East Allington)

Now stands a dereliction amid field and copse

Where buzzards fly and summer evening spies the slinking fox.

One can almost taste the atmosphere amongst this ruin

Made more electric when low mists hang or gales blow in.

Where strong willed boys once use to tittle-tattle

And soldiers in wartime came and prepared themselves for battle.

There still stands the bell tower and chimneys tall,

Creaking stairs and long corridors,

Remembering tales told of ghostly figures gliding through

And the nightly tap, tap, tap, heard by all and made by, no one knew.

Gone are the classrooms, stone table, pool and courts

That once held vibrant boys not so eager to be taught.

Today a somber tranquillity is what you will find

Offering refuge to a different kind

As rabbit and badger cautiously come out to play

Replacing the human spirits of yesterday

Now the estates lament is like a slowly dying ember

Such a strong past yet so few who remember

Sad Waters

No idle river the Severn and one that can mangle,

At Bridgnorth in winter the flooding gets high

And banks where schoolboys intently angle

Will soon be abraded by water swirling by.

When people fall in the local lore is quick to tell

Currents drag you down and pin you under a ledge.

Only when the river falls do you pop up in the swell

And end up downstream caught in some farmer's hedge.

Going to Angelsey the Menai bridge is notorious,

For jumpers it comes so conveniently to hand.

Do n 't look for their bodies, nothing so laborious

Ten days later pick them up, north of Puffin Island.

Neither does the Wye suffer fools gladly.

Lost souls get trapped in the rivers deep silt,

Held down for days they decompose badly.

It's been known to make even police divers wilt.

Night Walk

A day walk upon Dartmoor is always a thrill

But a walk in the night time is an uplifting pill.

Treading boldly in darkness using compass and pace

Brings great satisfaction when you find the right place.

At Norsworthy Bridge walk north east up the track

If you miss the turn for the pool you will have to backtrack.

From Crazy Well Pool you can climb north to the leat

And swing left at the channel as it cuts through the peat.

Follow the stream until you hear the call

Of the roaring of a torrent down the leat's waterfall.

In descending be careful the terrain is not good

But your watery guide brings you into dark Stanlake wood.

In choosing a campsite you have to be careful and brave

Don 't sleep with your head resting on some lonely grave.

The woodland stretch to Norsworthy has many a varied way

And you'll see an abundance of wildlife to really make your day.

Dartmoor.

An enigma, open moor

Featureless yet full of diversity.

It draws one into uncertainty,

Yet one treads with surety

Across its peat laden floor.

Tors stand like towers of Babel

Where buzzards fly high

And small mammals vie

For rocky protection

As best they are able.

Harsh, bleak, frozen or wet,

Inviting, warm, even Golden,

Stillness or storm we are beholden.

A rolling landscape of such beauty

Lays us in the Almighty's debt.

Chapter Three

Poems for the Children

A fore Thought.

Bundles of fun

Infinite curiosity

Somebody's daughter, somebody's son.

They are everything but mediocrity.

Pattericks

There once was a boy named Patryk

Who with food loved to prod and to pick

He would only eat beans and never any greens

So sadly he looked really sick.

There was a young man we will call Jac

Who had a pain in his tooth he could not hac

Going to the dentist he had it extracted by an apprentice

So he ran away never to come back.

There was a man from Maine

Who went by the name of Chain.

He behaved quite crazy

But then his first name was Daisy

Which would be enough to drive anyone insane.

There once was a boy named Maksym

Who at four became really taxing,

He'd shout and he'd yell and create absolute hell

Just anything to stop his parents relaxing.

A Horses Tail

Whisk it this way whisk it that

Flicking flies is what it's at

Owner puts it in a plait

Can't flick flies well, would n 't move a gnat

Lift the tail, what are they at?

oh, splat splat splat.

Seven.

I like chips

I like beans

I like sauce

But hate my greens

I love science

I love art.

I love maths

But hate being smart

I want my dad

I want my mother

I want my sister

But not my elder brother

I can tell time

I can tell jokes

I can tell tales

But I dare n 't tell my folks

continued

continued

I like Mark

I like Kevin

I hate girls

But then I'm only seven

Pincer the crab

This is the story of Pincer the crab

He lived on a coral reef where nothing was drab.

One day climbing high while playing the buffoon

A giant wave swept him up and across the lagoon.

It dumped him on a island of two rocks and a tree

But back over the lagoon his own reef he could see.

He stepped into the water to scuttle his way back

When a voice from behind him said "lad don't do that."

"In the deep water between island and reef

Lurks a giant octopus and he'll give you grief."

The news came from a lobster, a new friend called Claud

Who said "walk over there and you'll surely be gnawed."

The next day while looking up, high into the sky

Pincer saw a seagull and thought, I wish I could fly.

But Claud forever careful said, "watch out for them too

For seagulls eat crabs so they could also eat you."

(continued)

Pincer the crab.(continued)

Soon our crab is playing, not looking at the sea

When he spies a young seagull standing under the tree.

"Look out Mr. Seagull" Pincer shouts with all his might

The seagull hops forward, the voice gave him a fright

Then right from behind him comes a very loud thump

A huge coconut landed and it did make him jump.

"You saved my life little crab I owe it to you

To grant you a favour, anything you want me to do."

Now Claud waking up stepped away from his rock

To see a seagull eating crab, oh what a shock

The lobster was sad to think of Pincer in pain

And even worse that he would never see him again.

High over the octopus a young seagull did fly

Then above the coral reef it swooped down from the sky.

It dropped the little crab to safety, to mum

So Pincer did n 't end up in anybody's tum.

Baby Tales

When we awoke from our sleep

The day was calm and bright

And gazing up into the sky

We saw a very strange sight

The sun was shining warm and clear

Over our garden shed

But above our hedge the moon was there,

Mum exclaimed, it forgotten to go to bed.

For it hung in the sky like a silver disc

And mums story is as follows

When the sun comes up the moon goes down

Once a day, every day including yes, tomorrow.

So when we next get up and look outside

We should see a dawn

Of sun going up and the moon in bed

No tricks to spoil our morn.

continued

continued

But my mums tale of a moon in bed

Is for babes, not young men flush with science

As this young lad is now old enough,

To know her story has no reliance.

The top of our Christmas tree.

A beautiful December morn

Frost like icing on the lawn,

It 's time to get our decorations

A Christmas tree is to be born.

Excited searches of the loft

For boxes, bags and things,

Trundle it all down the stairs

Do n 't break the angels wings.

We build our tree from base to top,

It draws admiring glances

But wait, oh no, tragedy, guess what?

Someone's nicked the top three branches.

Searching high and searching low

They just cannot be found.

It 's all dads fault, he packed it up

Last xmas I'll be bound.

continued

continued

So Christmas starts for dad so sad

And with a tree that's so much shorter,

But by Christmas day he 's been forgiven

Even by his youngest daughter.

P.S. I have n 't got a daughter but sons does n 't rhyme.

Daddy Daddy

Bogey, bogey go away

Bogey, bogey I want to play

How can I play or be a singer

With you stuck on my middle finger

Daddy, daddy, I've done a pardon

I tried to go into the garden

But grabbing the door handle could not be done

With the bogey now stuck to my thumb

Daddy, daddy, look what I've stood in

Can you scrape it into the dustbin.

Oh daddy, daddy, please stay calm

The bogey is now stuck to my palm.

Daddy, daddy, can I have a drink

I've washed my hands in the kitchen sink.

If I tap my stomach it feels rather hollow

Though that bogey was quite hard to swallow.

continued

continued

Daddy, daddy, I don't feel well

I think my tummy has begun to swell

Do you have anything to treat it

I'll remember not to pick my nose and eat it.

Chapter Four

Poems about Life in the slow lane

A Fifth Thought

Everyone is becoming a hare and you the tortoise.

Inevitably, age or disability is slowing your purpose

But stay perky, resolved, have fun.

Don 't stagnate, worry, feel sorry and cuss.

The Silver Surfer

They coined a phrase not so long ago

The Silver surfer, yippee–i-o.

As a young man my passion was surf

So I looked forward one day to retirement, beach, waves, mirth.

Riding the tubes, wipe outs and such

Were terms of endearment needing bravado and luck.

Now retirements here I'm losing my hair

And doing my surfing from the old arm chair.

At twenty a short board, come fifty a keyboard,

So I'm surfing the web, not the waves with great flair.

Rise and Shine

When my son goes to sleep now he's older,

His mind must be roaming for he turns over and over

And when he wakes up, he remains in a daze

Because he drifts through the house as if in a maze.

Give him directions for every step that he takes

Washing, eating no difference it makes.

Unless you guide him through his very first hour

He's as bright as a light bulb without the power.

With boldness in dreams his thoughts must travel far,

For on waking his brain has been left on some star.

With mind adrift and his body in gear

One must direct every move, thank god he can hear.

Flabby Tabby

The old cat though timid and frail

Was quite cunning, though a small female.

Her immediate problem this early dawn

Was the flabby tabby from just next door.

This bossy tom had grown big and fat

By robbing the food of neighbouring cats.

He would lay close by and lick his paw

'Til he heard the chink of china upon the floor.

Then through the cat flap he would squirm

To eat the old ones food, - what an awful worm.

The food all gone he would squeeze on out

Getting fatter every day by dining out.

To get rid of the thief there had to be a simple way

And she saw the light after being sick one day.

It was not a problem to bring back what was eaten

Regular fur ball regurgitation being the reason.

continued

continued

Now the flabby tabby on his next stealing caper

Found food off the plate and on a newspaper

But on eating it all he received a bad stomach ache

So he never again returned to the old cats plate.

Ratchet Man

From 40 fit and fast times beginning to tell

I'm 50 fat and festering and really not all that well.

Parkies crept in at 48 But unlike some others

I haven't got the shakes.

It tripped me up and slowed me down

It's put me on hold slammed on the brakes.

So I pop the pills to move my stiff bones

But I find it depressing as I 'm putting on stones

My joints are much stiffer I go as fast as I can

If I were a super hero yes, I'd be ratchet man.

I know what to do to live a long life

The buffs keep on telling me giving me strife

But the spirits not willing to gear up a cog

To knuckle on down to diet and jog

So my lifestyles not right

But the bells of doom do not knell

However, I'm still fifty, fat and festering

And time is beginning to tell.

continued

continued

So I'll jump on my bike I'll go for a swim,

Get a rowing machine an exercise gym.

The garden gets dug

The dustbin gets cleared

The dishes get washed

The hedges get sheared.

So all is not lost

My head is not bowed

And I still get a laugh

When my son farts out loud.

Ratchet Man Five years on.

Well I'm still here so it can't all be bad

Though I'm slower, I stagger and I'm still a bit mad

At the waste of my life. What I wanted to do

Really was to roll on the floor and wrestle my boys

To take them on Dartmoor, bivi, wake up in the dew.

To the good I am lighter, fitter and have a sound diet

The boys are growing up, what happened to peace and quiet.

But don't get me wrong it's not something I dwell on

It's just something I miss, my fortune, so I'm going to get on.

I still have ambition such as paddle my canoe

And get my weight down to fifteen stone two.

To see the two youngest develop and blossom

And in the near future learn to wipe their own bottoms.

To Die or not to Die.

(That is the Question)

Has the time come to say good bye,

To call it a day, to do and die.

For keeping my dignity is top of the ladder

But more and more I can't control my bladder.

And I fear more what may come to pass

When eventually I can't wipe my own ass.

Why should others do these things for me

What is growing old without any dignity.

Being a burden to family or state

Is something I know I'll really hate

All my life I have kept body whole,

I've prided myself on self control.

So if I' m not to be in charge

I'll not be a burden to those at large.

And when the time comes to say goodbye

It will be thank you, good night, I choose to die.

Ten years on

A decade down the line with life's unexpected quirks

It's harder to keep my balance

And more of my movements now come in jerks.

The time between pills to delay the onset of my ills

Is definitely getting shorter,

At least by a quarter.

If I had a wish list on it I would scribe

To be a lot steadier, a better support for my wife.

I always take my medicine before driving the tribe

So not to mar my journey in the car

As in driving I'm still better than my wife,

To whom I owe all my happiness in life.

The doctor made his forecast

You have from five to twenty years

Of a fairly normal life but slow not fast.

Well I'm half way there

Still with zest and motivation a plenty

And quietly determined to do another twenty.

Chapter Five

Poems in a blast from the past

Thought Number Six

Thinking back over your time

Brings pleasure if not bliss

But remember the positive

Not just what you miss

Rugby for me

Jock Campbell was a big raw Scot

Who taught me rugby like as not

To carry the ball across the line

To run, run forward no matter what.

We won our first school match by seventy six

But it wasn't that which gave me a fix

It was my flying tackle on their winger

Where we both landed on the cricket pitch.

Remember, remember the fifth of November

And I really don't want to knock it

But I had to scrum down my face rubbing on skin,

 Deep purple and brown, after fireworks had burned in a pocket.

For someone considered as bright as a mangle

I was intrigued that rugby is in fact all angles

And though I found maths an intellectual challenge

The game never got me in any such tangle.

continued

continued

As the school seasons went on and on
I tried all positions from eight down to one
But for influence and control over the play
It was a back row shirt I chose to don.
For playing many clubs over hills and dales
For turning out in weather from sun to gales
For all the satisfaction playing rugby entails
It's a big thank you to the men of Wales.

Postcard to Louth

Well at least you left me the sofa and chairs,

The toaster, kettle and ironing board.

I suppose you could not get them down the stairs

And you didn't want the dog's chair with a leg half gnawed.

It was certainly a surprise when I returned

To find an empty apartment devoid of emotion.

No familiar smell of coffee or toast half burned,

Would you consider returning for my complete devotion.

Demise of a chair

Its seven years now since we came together

Since you first sat down, cotton on leather.

You snuggled into me many times a day

How can you be so heartless and throw me away.

All this time you've pressured me, given me form

How can you replace me, make me feel so forlorn.

You will take me to the tip, yes leave me in the lurch

Never a seat for your bottom, I'll be a seagulls perch.

A face from the past.

It's long ago now I find it so sad to say

That I can remember so little, about your manner, your way.

But I remember an instance where we used to meet

In the café in town just off the high street.

I waited with a friend for you to come in

Sipping coffee called Rhumba my head in a spin.

You stepped through the door my heart thumped in my chest

To me you were all, oh such loveliness.

You had been for a hair do it was up like a hive

It enlightened your face, I nearly died.

That vision I've held forty years to this day

One glimpse from the past, here now and forever to stay.

Memories

I reckon you've got to be at least fifty to do this well,

That's to look back years into the past,

For faces and memories to weave their magic spell.

And let one wonder,what ever happened to..

Hoping they've had a good life prosperous and caring,

Then if you met them again what memories would you be sharing.

What I remember of school before I was eleven,

Well faces are difficult but playtime was heaven.

The loo was a bucket and books were of slate,

But in all my days at school not one did I hate.

First Contact

A mercury flat fjord, not a wisp of wind

My kayak sat still, balanced between paddle and chine.

Nothing broke the silence

But I knew he was watching from right behind.

Did it have a memory of a time in the past

When the contact signalled a different intent.

Was it thinking don't get close,

Just in case a winged barb is chillingly sent.

We played a game for ten minutes or so

I would encroach and it would disappear

Quietly searching, patiently waiting,

It would always rise silently twenty yards to my rear.

A faint buzz in my ears then ended our time

A boat passed in the distance, the spell broke.

The whale sank into the deep

But my first contact, - sublime.

My Fallen Friend

I was in your brother's platoon

Just behind him that afternoon,

When they hit us with all they'd got

And your Dave took the first shot.

But I can say he didn't suffer at all

He passed away before he finished his fall.

Right up to that point he'd been caring and brave

The best example of how soldiers should truly behave.

I can't really imagine how you must feel,

But I hope this letter will help some small deal

When you know his many friends also feel your pain.

We pray that his death won't have been totally in vain.

Chapter Six

Poems

About

What gets up my nose

Thought Number Seven

The abuse of power is the single worst crime humanity commits,

While everyone has power politicians wield chunks of it, not little bits.

So one should not ignore them but note what they do,

And stand up and be counted when they start acting like doggy, doggy doo.

The Hedge

The back garden is looking lush and green

Though it's not summer but a deep winter scene.

The arbor shorn of entwined wisteria

Absorbs the wind's blowing like gusts of hysteria.

Fast grows the neighbour's leylandii hedge

Blocking the distant view to moor and sedge.

No matter how many red sunsets are desired

The golden rays of evening can never be admired

One can hope for a stroke of outlandish chance,

Say a fire or disease needs to lead a merry dance

Across the green wall now sixteen feet high,

Because if not stopped shortly it will soon reach the sky.

Two pigeons sit at the bird baths edge

Water for the residents of the imposing hedge

At least if I'm not happy with the evergreen curtain

Butterflies and birds are that's for certain

The News Reported. December.6.2001

Today, for us, the war stopped in Afganistan.

We didn't hear about bombs, starving children or any dead civilian.

Today our countries domestic issues were pushed to the fore.

Standards in parliament, conflict between our leaders

Inter party politics can be a bore.

Not that it's unimportant and shouldn't be news

But when humanity is dying

Deciding what's a priority to publish, what to choose

Is a great responsibility for the person in the editor shoes.

Two days later the news returned to Kabul

About last stands and friendly fire

So it made you wonder if there had been a lull.

But you knew in your soul it hadn't been a priority to be reported

And that the bombing and killing hadn't really been aborted.

The man from Texas.

There once was a man from Texas

Who when he became President could only vex us

He started a war by lying more and more

It was like being hit in our soft solar plexus.

He went after the head of Iraq

In one overwhelming superior attack

He captured the man, said well done everyone

And declared the war over, job done and that's that.

But his policies lacked planning and precision

Were not thought through with a clear sense of vision

Innocent people were killed, and freedom fighters instilled

With a sense of purpose on the right of their mission.

Now to get out of his mess it's the U.N. he should bless

Letting middle and far east peacekeepers take over

The U.S. could pay for the lot from their deep money pot

And he could still come up smelling like clover.

Watch for the vultures

Distressed animal where

Distressed animal there

Circle closer

Cease to hover land quite near

Creature harmless no need to fear.

Dart in, tear, run off with a morsel

The Victim, like one lone food parcel.

Law of nature

Don't show any anguish

Or you will become the vulture's next prime dish.

Coping

He choked. His thoughts, even they stuttered

He had to lean on the wall emotionally gutted.

Bereavement had n't been included throughout his years

Now a tsunami of loss surged through him, destroyed were his peers.

The loss of a good friend and then his wife's father,

Now his younger sister which made it harder and harder.

Where was the order of things, the eldest go first

Mums and dads then children once grown should follow in the hearse.

The cramp in his mind makes him unable to respond

To the close family and friends of the one they were all so fond.

On the phone his throat freezes, and what can one say

He can never find adequate words to express and convey.

He has learnt to deflect some of the pain and saddness

By choosing happy memories to bring him some gladness

Though time is the great healer his mother had once said

Memories still creep up and smack him on the back of his head.

Ode to the would be Hack

If the pen is to be mightier than the sword

Then learn to use well, the written word.

It is not in what you say, but in how,

That will make your pen mightier than even the plough.

If a picture paints a thousand words

Then buy one of Jackson Pollocks,

For the photograph seems king today

Most portraying boobs and bollocks.

The written word gives a depth of feeling

On subjects from heaven to hell,

While photographs of a catastrophe fall short

They cannot describe the sense of smell.

Your column should pronounce the facts

Not the fairytales made up by tabloid hacks

Let your copy be profound, caring, a loud voice

For remember the pen is your weapon of choice.

Chapter Seven

Thoughts and Poems About Sonnets

Thought number eight On Sonnets

Ever thought about writing a sonnet?
The bard wrote one hundred and fifty four
So probably had a bee in his bonnet
About this type of poem: and oh there's more
Keep to ten syllables a line, or near;
Finish at the end of the fourteenth line;
Write about everything you hold most dear
Not forgetting every other line must rhyme.
He wrote about love, his life and the weather
Passions, in a sixteenth century history:
Yes, the last two lines should rhyme together
His great touch was that sense of mystery
And then his obvious gift of the gab,
Which is much more than I will ever have.

A Sonnet from George

A vision guides my siege mentality

It's I am the corporate war monger

And control the oil, no banality.

I am not one who relieves world hunger.

We will impose our values on you all

And we will do whatever it may take,

Believe us, gods' with us, we have the gall.

Remember we do not negotiate.

So what if we contradict ourselves; like

 We are Pro life but war kills dads and wives.

The message from the President's psyche

Is never help other countries lives

Or clean the environment up a notch,

Because these things don't happen, on my watch.

A Legacy

(Boxing Day 2004)

Jewel of the universe, planet so blue,

Your beauty belies an awesome trait

That nature can without warning make due,

Annihilation from the slip of a plate.

So to people on one twelfth of the globe

With a huge sweep of your watery hand

You wiped away a million abode

Burying all in sea, rubble and sand.

But in ripping out humanities soul

There may yet come a legacy so bold

For humans are but one family, one whole.

Support and sharing is the key, our gold.

Harmony can come if we remember

With compassion the grief of that December.

Glossary

Arbor.   A shady enclosure formed by trees.

Abraded.   Worn away

Bivi.   A temporary shelter

Chine.   The backbone of a kayak.

Chop.   Vivisection.

Fogey.   A dull old person.

Jacek.   Pronounce Yassek

Leat   Man made channel carrying water.

Loo   Lavatory Mangle A rolling press to squeeze out water from linen

Moreish   Such that one wants more.

Parkies `   (Colloquial) for Parkinson's Disease

Patteryks   As Limericks but based on the brothers of Patryk

Plate   As in geological tectonic plate in earth movement

Rhumba   Coffee beverage laced with rum

Trundle   To roll along.

About the Author

- Born 1947,Educated Loughborough College School. England. Trained as a teacher. Taught in Modern, Grammar, Comprehensive, Further Education and Special Needs establishments. Found teaching special needs children the most rewarding. Interests mainly on the active side – Royal Marine Reserve, Rugby and Sea Kayaking. Diagnosed with Parkinsons Disease in 1994. Now retired, living in Devon from where he keeps an eye on his six sons.